Poems From the Strange Mind of Me:
Love and other possibly icky things

W. M. Stahl

For the women that inspired me to open myself and let these words out from within me.

W. M Stahl

This is simply a collection of poems that I have written over the years and in various places around the United States. I offer it up to you the reader, so that it may give you a little escape from your day, week or hour. I by no means offer them up so that someone somewhere can tear them apart and analyze them or my intent in writing them. Yet perhaps someday someone will and for those I say... don't. Spare yourself the trouble, as there is no underlying purpose or reason to how I have written them or why.

I have spent several months trying to decide if I would offer the following poems to the world to read for whatever purpose or reason I have as you can tell come to the conclusion to do just that. Some have been shared and viewed by many of my friends and family many more still have ever been only seen by me and their intended receiver. While about five of them have been previously been published in anthologies I am fairly sure no one but those that had poems in them ever bought or received copies of the books. Some have even made themselves seen on my website titled From The Strange Mind of Me. I have broken them down into two categories such as they are, while I have done that I have not put them in any kind of order other than that, at least not intentionally. Perhaps some of you may not agree that what lies within these pages is in fact poetry. Truth is you may have something there. What makes a group of words a poem; rhymes, rhythm, passion sentiment, or something else entirely? There are several accepted forms of poetry for sure but if you look back in time at epic prose and early accepted poems they seem to have little in common with what is accepted as poetry today and more in common with stories fact and fiction. Still does that make them less a poem? As you can well guess I am not the person to ask that question as I believe that poetry is poetry in whatever form you find it. Whether you find it in rhyme, rhythm, passion, sentiment or something else entirely I believe it can still be called poetry. Whether or not I agree with what they hold in verse and I may in fact dislike the form that is the poem I do not contend to say that it is not poetry. Admittedly some of the poems you will find within are perhaps corny and repetitive in nature and verse. Yes I could have taken them out or fixed them however, many of the poems within were written at the spur of the moment. To change them now would, in my opinion, perhaps change the passion and sentiment in which they were written.

That being said I do hope that you spend a minute and enjoy them, perhaps you will smile at one and tear at the next and wonder what I was thinking in the next. Either way I hope that you are entertained in your trip through the Strange Mind of Me.

W. M Stahl

Love

Poems and Other Possibly Icky Things

It is It

There is nothing as powerful as it
Everything in our lives is ruled by it
It runs our lives and we keep track of it
We are conceived of it
We are born of it
We are raised with it
We are made sick by it
We are broken by it
We are cared for by it
We are cured with it
Yet we search for it
We crave it
We miss it
We live for it
We desire it
We hate it
We loath it
We act crazy for it
We are driven crazy by it
We even die from it
Yet it is all of what life is
Without it we are nothing
Nothing else will do
For us love is it

Wait for Love

Love comes to those who wait
So they say and so we wait
Day after day we still wait
For love to come; and yet its wait
Its winter now, no bodily warmth, oh just wait
Flowers of spring all new, oh no still wait
The summer heat and yet we wait
Fall comes and its colorful splendor but wait
How long can it go on, this wait
To hell with this too long of a wait
I've waited too long now this wait
Just turns into more weight

Words

Words can mean so much
Words spoken mean so much more
But to me
If they are not spoken
Or written for you
To hear or read
They are just meaningless words
Words of love are just words
Until they are returned
Open the door to your world
I will open my door to you
Open your heart to me
I will open my heart to you
Open the door to your world
I will open my world to you
Open your eyes to me
I will open my eyes to you
Open your heart to me
I will open my heart to you
Open your soul to me
I will open my soul to you
Words of love are just words until they are returned
I send you these words so that you will see
That without you they are just words on a page

Come to Me

Come to me in the morning
With your breath so soft
Come to me in the morning
Lay your body next to mine

Let me kiss your lips
All trembling and soft
Let me kiss your lips
Until nothing matters but us

Your body shivers
But you are not cold
Your body shivers
Touching you calms you

Come take my hand
We will come together
Come take my hand
We can do anything together

W. M Stahl

My dreams of ever after

Just as I breathe
So do I dream
Just as I am
So do I dream

It is in my dreams
That I am happiest
To live as I dream
Would make me the happiest

To dream of you
Is to dream of ever after
To dream of you
Is to dream of life after

In my dreams
There is only you
In my dreams of ever after
There is only you

Time to Dream

With time to dream of anything
All I can do is dream of you
Suffering through yet another day
It is yet another day without you

I meet you in my dreams for a reason
For all the reasons that I can
If but for a brief moment you come to me
It is a good enough reason to dream

With time to dream of anything
It is all I can do to not dream of you
I have given into the pressures
And yet it is another day without you

I meet you in my dreams for a reason
For it is the only way that I get to see you
Your face and body escape me every time
But it is still a good enough reason to dream

Suffering through yet another day
I lay down each night and wait
Somewhere in the night you arrive
It is all I can do to dream of you

If but for a brief moment you come to me
It is enough that you come
Dreaming of you is a good reason
But I dream for all the reasons that I can

Surrender

How is it done this surrender
Do I wake one day
To say that this is the day
This is the day of my surrender
It is said that that it's the only way
The only way to know is to surrender
They say there are signs everywhere
It matters not where you look there they are
Is it really just fate and destiny after all
Could this be just written all in some book
Our life written before it has begun
The where and with who written down
Could that be true in a world like this
Enough of that where was I
Surrender to love to know love
Or so they have always said
It is said that you never truly know it
If in fact it ever comes your way
It is not the mind that it occurs
But only in the heart
That it must be surrendered to
For only if we surrender do we learn
Surrender your heart and soul
For it is only then that will we discover love

To Make you Happy

I wish I could cheer you up with a thousand kisses
Just to make you happy
If I could I would give you the moon
If only you would be happy
I would send to you a million bouquets of flowers
If only it would make you smile
I would chase the devil from his throne
If only it would make your day
I would sing you every song that I know
If only you would be in a better mood
So many things I would do
If only they would make you
I wish that I could make you happy
But I can only tell you that I am here
On the chance that I can make you happy

Eyes and Soul

If you were to look into my eyes and see my soul
What would your eyes say to me
If you were to look into my eyes and see my soul
What would your heart say to you
If you were to look into my eyes and see my soul
Would you see your soul
If you were to look into my eyes and see my soul
Would you see your heart
If you were to look into my eyes and see my soul
Would you see what I see
If you were to look into my eyes and see my soul
Would you see my love for you
If you were to look into my eyes and see my soul
Would you accept my love for you
If you were to look into my eyes and see my soul
Would you see that we were meant for each other

Be my Jewel

Come to me
Come be my Jewel
Come dressed in black
Come with sunlight in your hair

Your emerald eyes searching
Your hands waiting to be held
Your lips longing for a kiss
Your body waiting to be held

I am here for you
I have love to give
I am waiting for you
I need only you to live

Dreams can come true
Dreams of happiness rule us
Dreams of family
Dreams that only love can satisfy us

Come be my jewel
Your emerald eyes searching
I am able to love and care
Dreams can come true

Best Love

I wake each day with you
Your breath soft in my ear
Hands resting gently on my chest
Fingers curl and uncurl unconsciously
My arm pulls you closer
You sigh as you settle back in
Your new place on my chest quiets you
Tilting your head slightly you kiss my neck
It is one of the many things I love about you
Then I realize it is all in my dreams yet again
And still it makes no difference
Even my dreams tell me what I need to know
Telling me over and over that our love is real
In sleep or awake ours is the best love

Always

I feel you in my sleep
You must be dreaming of me
I feel you in my waking moments
You must be walking with me on your mind
I feel you as I go off to work
You must be holding me in your mind
I feel your presence as I work
You must be talking to me in your thoughts
I feel you when I come home
You must be welcoming me home to you
I feel you as I lay down to sleep
You must be holding me in your mind
I feel you always
You must be thinking of me as I think of you
Always

Open Hearts

When I look at you I see everything
Your world is wide open for me to see
All I need is your loving touch
To let me know that you are mine
I stand with my heart open for you to see
All that I am and all that I can be
I offer it to you to keep forever
I hope that you will not let it go ever
Keep it close to yours and hold it tight
In time they will beat together as one
Know that it means so much to me
After all it is my only heart
Keep it as close to as you can
Hold it close to your heart
I open my heart to you
That you want it near yours
As I want yours near mine
Without you I know no love
With you I know all I need
That you are mine and I am yours
Open your heart to mine
As mine is open only for you

I Wake

I wake to find my love
Her skin soft and warm
Her lips dry from sleep
I wonder if I should kiss them wet
Or wait until she wakes
She sleeps so soundly
Her gentle breath deep
I do not want to wake her
Yet I want so much to wake her
To kiss her awake
To turn her dry lips wet
I want to look into her eyes
I want to see them blink open
To see the first light in her eyes
To be the first thing she sees
As close to heaven as a man can get
Kiss me my love
Open your eyes on mine
Be the light of my day
And the light of my life

Tender Flower

Far away is the flower of love
Words of love fly across the wires
Far away is the flower of love
Back and forth so that they will discover
Far away is the flower of love
What the other is seeking
Far away is the flower of love
Words on the screen appear
Far away is the flower of love
Melting the heart of the one it is meant
Far away is the flower of love
Just as the snow melts to reveal its secrets
Far away is the flower of love
Tender is the flower that is seeking love

I Reach To The Clouds

I reach to the clouds and carry you
In this dream there is room for us both
The wind that blows is but the love
The clouds are under our feet
The clouds hold us up in the sky
They are the base of our love

I reach to the clouds to protect you
In this life to keep you safe from harm
The wind that blows will suffice
And serve to make a path of long love
In this sky we will live forever
Happy in our world of love and children

I reach to the clouds and bring you to me
In this the only love that can keep us
Together we live
Together we create
The wind that blows will carry us
Across the divide and on forever

I reach to the clouds take my hand
Together we will give to each other
In this life that is all love
Where only two can truly be happy
Together we will live
None that join us could be as happy as we

I reach to the clouds and carry you
I reach to the clouds to protect you
I reach to the clouds and bring you to me
I reach to the clouds take my hand
I reach to the clouds give me all of you
I reach to the clouds and we will be one

If I Could Fly

If I could fly
It would be nothing really
There would be no distance
That would separate
It would be an easy thing
If I could fly

Fly to your arms
And never leave them
That is what I would do
Nothing would keep me away
It would be an easy thing
If I could fly

Flying is easy they say
When you're in love
It's the falling that hurts
When there is no love returned
It would be an easy thing
If I could fly

In Your Eyes

In your eyes I see your smile
and I can see your life
In your eyes I see your smile
and I can live

I look to your eyes
and in them you are lonely
I look to your eyes
and in them you are happy

I can see past your eyes
and see the person that you are
I can see past your eyes
and see the beauty that is you

I look deep in your eyes
and see the children you will have
I look deep in your eyes
and see the mother you will be

The way the light strikes your eyes
makes me want to be that light
The way the light strikes your eyes
makes me want to live in the reflection

I look deep into your eyes
and see the way the light strikes them
I look deep into your eyes
and in them I can see your smile

I look to your eyes
and I can see your soul
I look to your eyes
and I could love you forever

Kisses

Kisses so soft and sensual
The taste of your sweet lips
Drives me to want more
Gentle caress of your hand
Fingers lightly touching my skin
Driving me out of my mind
To feel your touch is to finally be fee
To kiss you is to taste for the first time

My Comfort

The comfort of my day
Is when I see her
The comfort of my day
Is when she is near

To see her name
As it appears on my screen
To see her name
With the heart next to it

I call her my bunny
And yes even my honey
I call her my bunny
She makes my heart feel oh so funny

For all the many ways
That she makes my day
Only my bunny is
The comfort of my day

My Love

My love is a flower that blooms
My love is a sun that rises
My love is the moon that fills the night sky
But mostly my love is you
For you bloom all year long
With the brightness of the sun
And with the fullness of the moon
Filling my life with your scents
And brightness that lights my gloom
Filling my heart over and over
My love is life that fills me
Turning my darkness to light
With beauty and delicate scents
Your soft light glows from within
Lighting my life with your presence
My love makes my spirit soar
Carrying me to new heights
Everyday a new adventure
To keep me from my boredom
My love is everything that is life
You lift me from myself
To show me what life is worth
Yes you do all these things
For you are my love

My new Heart

Your hair shimmers in the sun
Your eyes sparkle in the shade
Your fingers gently entwined
Your heart beats with mine

As we walk I wish for you to see
As we walk I wish for you to know
As we walk I wish for you to feel
As we walk I wish for you hear

My smile is wider when you are near
My day is happier when you are near
My world is larger when you are near
My life complete when you are near

You say that you want to make me happy
I say that you need only to love me
You say that you want to be happy
I say that you need only to love me

I say to you, open your heart
I say to you, you need only to love me
I say to you, you need just to be
Open your arms and you will find my new heart

Your Smile

Smiles form dimples in your cheeks
They keep me coming back for more
It is your smile that makes you more beautiful
To kiss and hold you is my quest
To stroke your hair and cheek as you smile
To see your eyes as they sparkle and tell of your love
Just to gaze in your face is to see my life
Crushing you to my body just to be closer
Your soft breath in my ear as I hold you close
Your exhale warm and deep
The sound of love that escapes with it
Your touch brings a shiver to me
I do not know why it does but I cannot stop
Kissing me you tell me all is well as I taste your sweet breath
Telling me you are mine without words
Kiss me again my love so that I may breathe again

Your Beautiful Face

I look at your beautiful face
wondering who you are
I look at your beautiful face
wondering how you are
I look at your beautiful face
and I see the beauty that is inside
I look at your beautiful face
and I see all that is burning to be outside
I look at your beautiful face
and I want it close to mine
I look at your beautiful face
and I wonder what kind of wife you will be
I look at your beautiful face
and I wonder what kind of mother you will be
I look at your beautiful face
and I see all
I look at your beautiful face
and I want all
I look at your beautiful face
and I can no longer hold back my passion
I look at your beautiful face
and I can no longer hide what is becoming obsession
I look at your beautiful face
and I want to watch you
I look at your beautiful face
and I want to watch as you experience your desires
I look at your beautiful face
and I want to see your face in pleasure
I look at your beautiful face
and I want to see the tears of joy
I look at your beautiful face
and realize that I want to look at you
For the rest of my days

Speak of Love

To speak of love
Is to speak of life
It is an old story
This one of love

We whisper its name
We praise its character
We desire it more than fame
We praise the feeling

What is this love
Stories are told of it
It's sought after more than gold
Lives lived for only for it

We whisper its name
Over and over to ourselves
Liking how it rolls off our tongue
It gives us warmth to think it

How does this work
Why speak it only in whispers
Why not shout to the world
Would the search be easier

To let all know when we seek it
To let all know when we find it
We let all know when it is real
Sharing it having found the one

It is all a mystery
Yet we still speak the words
Whispering or shouting they come out
Those powerful words of love

Thoughts of you

Words that I speak
But only in whispers
Keep me in thought
From night until day

Visions of my love
Run rampant in my head
Until I cannot tell
Dream from reality

Words that I speak
But only to myself
Keep me talking
From day until night

Conversations with you
Keeping me calm
While you are there
And I am here

Visions of my love
Run through my mind
Keeping me in thought
Until I can dream again

Every Day

Into my life
You have come
Into my life
You will stay

In my arms
You are always needed
In my arms
You will always be welcome

I am glad
We have met
I am glad
Even though we are far apart

I need you
At the start of my day
I need you
At the end of my day

In my mind
Is where I keep you
In my mind
Is where I dream you

One more time
We are apart on this day
One more time
I must tell you by letter

I love you
On this Valentine's day
I love you
On every day in between

Cupids Warmth

Winters cold wind still blows
Snow piles up to the windows
January thaw not so far behind
Yet huddling together keeping warm
It comes again and again as it always does
That feeling that holds on to me forever
Your head on my arm while sleeping lightly
Gentle breathing keeps my arm warm
Could this be what I have waited for all along
This closeness in body and heart
Once a year it comes like most important things
A lover's day through the night and the next
Soon it will be time to part
Reality comes again as it always does
Holding on to each other
Never wanting to leave the moment
Or for the moment to ever end
Stay hidden just an hour more
Trying to escape that which always comes
Hold me closer today than any other
Remind me that you love me this day
And all the of the days between this until next
Come my love share this day with me
Cupid is in our world this day that we may know
That our love is stronger now than last he was here
Happy Valentines my love
May we feel this love all through the year

All I Want

I have thought all day
of all the ways
and what to say
on this Valentine's Day

I have thought of how much
of all the touches
and every other such
on this we think very much

I can only say to you my honey
of all the things that cost me money
and makes me laugh and think you funny
on this day all I want is you my bunny!

On This Day

On this day of love
I ask for your loving touch
There is nothing without it
I ask for your loving touch

I come to you with empty arms
For you to fill as only you can
I come to you with an empty heart
For you to fill as only you can

Step into my arms and fill them
Let me feel you there
Come into my heart and it
Let me feel you there

On this day of love
All I need is your loving touch
I am empty without your love
All I need is your loving touch

W. M Stahl

Addicted

Her big soft brown eyes sparkle
Each time she looks my way
Her face waiting to be held
With lips crying out 'kiss me' after each word
Her short sweet body begging to be held
Silent words every time she moves
She whispers come love me
Without saying a word
Deep black hair hangs over her face
Keeping her in mystery
Soft brown eyes sparkle
Each time the candle flickers
Makes it hard to look anywhere else
Each smile brings out her dimples
The crinkle in corners of each eye
Tells me each time I dare to look
She is happy just to be across from me
Holding her white rose as a prize
Soon she will tell me of her day
The rose will not dip once as she speaks
Each word that comes out hangs in the air
As if it does not want to leave mouth
A happy sound follows each sentence
But only I can hear it
I am not sure what she is saying
I can only hear the happy sound
All I can see are her eyes sparkling
And her lips as they make her happy sound
I am done I am hers and she is mine
I lean in to hear her better
But I know I do not care what she says
There's nothing I can do I am addicted

Good Night

Goodnight my love
My dreams call to me now
Telling me that you wait for me there
I will kiss you there
In my dreams as I always do
It is there that I know you will be
And there that I can always find you
For you my love I wait to be together
One day we will be I know
If only in my dreams

Eyes of Green

Colors of green draw me in
Emerald colored eyes haunt me
Making me wish for new things
The old is no longer good enough
I must move ahead to stay alive
Yet slow enough so I am not in too deep
Blinding smiles keep me coming back
But no longer have the same effect
And still the struggle continues as always
One step ahead five steps behind
It is imperative that I am always vigilant
Just to keep it all separate

As you walk

As you walk so go I
When you stumble I will help
As you feel so do I
When you hurt I will help

In your darkest times
I will be there for you
In your lightest times
I will be there for you

When you need a hand
You need only call out
When you just need an ear
You need only call out

If you stumble
Lean on me
If you hurt
Take my strength

When you are down
I will lift you up
Call on me my friend
Whenever you need

Fleeting Feelings

Back in the day way, way back
When we were young and full of life
There was life yet to live before now
And still there were songs to be sung

Time went by quickly without knowing
Where did it all go this time of our feelings
Did the feelings go or was it time that went
Slipping away from us like so many things

Back in the day when we were young
When we were young and full of life
There was life yet to live and songs to be sung
We stood tall and proud so young and full of life

Time went by too quickly and unknowingly
Where did they all go these feelings in time
Did the time pass first or the feelings
Slipping away without truly knowing

Back in the day way back in our past
When we were so young and a full life ahead
There was so much life for us to live
And still when there was so many songs to sing

Time went by before we could stop it
Where did it go it's hard to say but we lived it
Did the time kill the feeling or feelings kill the time
Slipping away just the same it's all fleeting feelings

Love rebuked

Soft turning bodies on a summer night
Twisting turning under the moon light
Kisses secretly given in the darkness
Passions mixing and mingling
Forged only behind closed doors
Once forbidden always forgiven
Always in the dark never in the light
Hour after hour huddled together
Living in a separate world
While everyone else lived theirs
Reality kept away once together
Together kept away when apart
Never noticing the other
Always knowing the other is near
Notes passed in passing
Passing by as an answer
Calls made in silence
Always answered in code
Loudly ringing in the mind
Never the same time
Always the same place
Things are always said
And life never gives up the chase
Reality crashes every party
Worlds have ways of coming together
Hiding only prolongs the search
And the search only prolongs the hiding
A love once given is a love once taken
A love no more to be shared
Love rebuked is a love no more
Perhaps a love that never was
Only a sensation of pleasure
Soon pain replaces pleasure
Before long hatred replaces pain
But not of the love just the loss of it

Thoughts of them too painful
Thoughts that were shared
Feelings that were given and taken
False feelings really
True feelings never die
Who is to say what is or what was
After all love is just a theory

Deep Feelings

Deep feelings of love
Keep me going on day after day
Pouring down on me like rain from above
Seeping into my heart in every way

Partial thoughts keep blocking my mind
So hard to keep things straight
So easy to get behind
These thoughts will have to wait

Deeper things have taken control
In my mind where nothing always makes sense
They double and triple before reaching their goal
All this does nothing but make me tense

Could this be the way it always happens
These deep feelings of love that grow
Once around and through the mind
Keeping me from keeping it all straight

Day after day it happens
In one side and around to the other
Deeper it goes caring not of my mind
Doing nothing but keeping thinking

Soon I will have little choice
Something will have to be done
Soon these deep feelings will take over
Running in and around my heart

Sleep

With closed eyes to fall asleep
Fighting somewhere between light and darkness
A quick shake to stay awake
Because its sleep that brings the dreams

Whipping away at tired watery eyes
Anything to keep it at bay a little longer
Caffeine that no longer works
Just in time to see the sunrise yet again

It is only the body that craves sleep
The mind knows little difference
Yet still I shake once then twice
Soon I know I will not be able to stop it

The need will overcome me
I will slip off into sleep
No matter how hard I shake
I will begin to crave it

Too hard to keep moving
If I just close my eyes for a second
Another shake and I am awake
Am I really awake or is this the dream

A quick shake to stay awake
Why do I shake to stay awake
It is the sleep that brings the dreams
And the dreams that bring only you

Poems and Other Possibly Icky Things

Other Possible Icky Things

W. M Stahl

Words in the Wind

Wind through the trees echoes
Carrying whispers from days before
Listen closely for the stories as they pass
Words lump together in clumps like leaves on trees
Finding their way onto pieces of paper
Some continue on out and over the fields
Only to be caught by someone else
In some other place or time
Words in the wind carry out over time
From place to place to be caught and used
While others slip past going farther on
Rolling on for others to catch their whispers
Whispers of words lumping together
Forming the stories we read when all together
Words in the wind come again and again
Carry the words to the days after us
So that others that follow can use them
Making the stories yet to be told

The Problem

Folded arms one over the other
Standing with legs spread wide
Disgust that covers your face
The choices were made too early
Too late now to change anything
Try not to see it just one way
Look from the other side too
Frustration quickly turns to anger
Too soon does judgment come
Turn away from it
Unfold your arms one from the other
Sit down to hear me out
I cannot have you standing there
In your judgmental stance
Seeing only your anger rising
Look to me to see what I see
See the other side of what you see now
Oh the hell with, it stay that way
What does it matter all considered
You would not believe me if I told you anyway
I should keep trying to get you to see
What is the use you will still be mad at me
No matter what I do or what I say
You will say I am an ass just the same
So to make this short and less bitter
I'll just kiss your ass now if it's all the same
Oh forget it I'll just sleep on the couch

W. M Stahl

Blah, Blah, Blah

Tell me something else
It is not like you really care
Tell it to someone else
What was that, not again

I always hear what you say
Yes so you have told me before
I said I always hear what you say
My god why don't you stop

Are you honestly talking again
What does it take to shut you up
Why are you talking again
Just once I wish you would stop

Why do I know you will continue
For crying out loud please stop
Oh no you just want to continue
Just once I want to make you stop

Why do you think I care
Sometimes I want to tell you
Oh do you even care
Yet Blah, Blah, Blah is all I really hear

Mothers

For mothers of sons and daughters
For mothers of mothers
For mothers of children yet unborn
For mothers of adults with their own

Those that we are born to
Those that we cling to
Those that we turn to
Those that we run to

For our up brining we own them
For our bumps and bruises they did kissed away
For our ups and downs that they were there for
For our lives as they watched over us

Giving to us our morals
Giving to us the ideas
Giving to us our attitudes
Giving to us the love

To mothers that have taken us in
To mothers that are mothers no matter who you are
To mothers that to us are not of our blood
To mothers that to us are only of law

Throughout our lives they will remind us
Throughout our lives they will answer
Throughout our lives they are there
Throughout our lives they are always there

Into their lives we have come
Into their lives we will grow
Into their lives we will be
Into their lives until they are gone

In our lives they will always be
In our lives they will poke their nose
In our lives they will always be
In our lives they will control

To mothers of sons and daughters
Those that we are born to
For our upbringing we owe them
Giving to us our morals

To mothers who have taken us in
Throughout our lives they will remind us
Into their life we have come
In our lives they will always be

From your sons and daughters that live and breath
From your sons and daughters that have gone before you
From your sons and daughters that you have yet to meet
From your sons and daughters that love you the most

Fathers

Father oh father
You are our strength when are in need
You are our knight in shining armor
You are the one that lifts us up when we have fallen
You are the one we look to when in need
In your eyes we find our strength
In your eyes we find our armor
In your eyes we find our way up
In your eyes we find our necessity

Have we Forgotten?

How to live and feel
Are we bound to walk unknowing
The warmth of the sun or the wetness of the rain
Even the gentle touch of the snowflake

How to embrace life and love
Its laughter and every tear
The soft kiss of a lover awakening
The smile of simple satisfaction

How to smell and taste
Not knowing the smell of a spring rain and lilacs through an
open window
A freshly mowed field of hay in the summer
The flavors of a summer harvest on a cool fall day

To open your mind and learn to live
Embrace each day as if it were the first and last
Smell the fragrance of each day and taste its harvest
To do this is to not forget

Too much

I think too much I think
If I would not think
I think I could sleep
If I could sleep
I would not think

Talk about a dilemma
If I talk at all
It surely would not be of that
I fumble for the light again
I find myself awake again

Late at night my mind spins
Thoughts of dreams
Dreams of thoughts
It gives to me nothing
Just more lines under my eyes

Early in the morning my mind spins
Busy with thoughts that I did not think
Although I must have brought them to mind
To think I have done so deliberately
Just to keep myself from sleeping

Train Set

With a rattle and a shake it would stop
Off the track again with a big hop
Twisting, and leaning from side to side
With shouts and woops from all at hand
The engine tilting barely hanging on
Workmen rushed quickly to the rescue
Safety of the rail depended on their work
The express would be coming way too soon
Pushing pulling the cars back onto the track
The cargo restacked on their cars
Passengers climb the steps once again
Taking their seats they wait to be going again
With a blast of its whistle the engine tells all
Soon all will be well and they will be off
Cheers filed the air as it would begin again
Across the field it went around the turn
Through the tunnel then past the factory
Slowing down it finally arrived in town
Down would come the arms to stop the cars
Crossing Main Street and the children waving
With its whistle blowing it would round the last turn
Breaks' squeaking as it comes to a stop
With a final look the passengers climbed slowly down
Into the station to be warmed or for a quick meal
Red capped men and women climb aboard
Sorting through they unload the proper luggage
With watch in hand the conductor paced back and forth
The dinner bell sounding in the background
With a groans and moans the engineer would finally rise
Stepping over the train sounding off their objections
Off to the dinner table with a pout on their lips
The express would just have to wait

Moonlit Dance

Dancing in the moon light
Feeling only the moment
Moving in small circles in the light
Savoring each and every moment
Swaying gently together in time
Only two can hear the soft music
Each step is one closer together
Moon light falls down around us
Breeze blows the scent of flowers
Filling all of our senses at once
Holding each other closer and closer
Stars overhead jealously looking down
A kiss stolen in the dance
The dancers become the lovers
The lovers become the dancers
Intertwined in the moon light
Looking down at your naked skin from above
It is the moon that is jealous now
Your beauty and smooth skin glowing
Reflecting the light of the moon
Suddenly the dance ends
Imaginary music heard only by two
Fading away in the coming daylight
All that will be left is just us two
Curled up beneath the fading star light
Unlike the moon the sun is never jealous
Only harsh and unforgiving
Hours from now the moon will return
So will the moonlit dance

W. M Stahl

Humor Imagination Irritation

Teens on the street
Disrespect for authority
Disrespect for each other
How does it begin
Where does it end

With laughter we move on
Past those that irritate us
Jokes made, dues are paid
Laughter not always covering
Jokes hold us from our anger

Teens in the hallway
Showing off the damage of words
Looking down hiding in the mind
Imagination hides the pain
Ignore everything but the brain

Choice one is to live in the mind
It is a far better place to be
Without is the words and acts
Those that hurt and disrespect
Never caring what the price will be

Young adults on the street
Adults in name only
Respect for others far away
Respect for themselves even farther
Disrespect has built the wall

Hate filled words
Once were just disrespectful
Fill the minds of those that think them
Spilling out as they speak
Irritation builds in those that hear them

Laughing at them is the only answer
Letting the words fall away
Is the best way to fight
Spoken in hate received by laughter
It is all useless if we show no sign

In our minds we are protected
Shielded from the words we go on
We can't go on in our mind forever
Time goes on life must still be lived
Irritations can be forgotten

All words mean something to someone
There are three that mean so much to us all
Irritation is that which bothers us
Humor is that which makes us laugh
Imagination is that which holds us together

Various Thoughts

Various thoughts flip through my mind
Connected disconnected each the same
All that really matters is the thought
Is life patterned after theory
Is theory patterned after life
Are they all truly the same
Waking each morning to a new day
Why can we not just awaken the same day
Relive the best day of our life over and over
Would that be a crime of time
Is there any one or thing that controls that
Ah sweet mystery of life it is come again
This thought of destiny and our role in it
The books of destiny written or not
Tis true a question of scholars
All smarter than I for sure
And yet even they do not know for sure
Or have they just not told us
Of politics I dare not write
Yet it seems that it is the interest of late
My mind might explode of those thoughts
So various of these that would spill from me
Surely my fingers would not keep up
And I am sure that my mind would explode
If by chance I could not get it out fast enough
So I think of everything else that would fit here
And come to a conclusion about my thoughts
They come and go as they please
Though many times I try to keep them straight
It matters not for all I can do is let them pass
On and through my mind one or more at a time
Good lord the things that happen in my mind
If I had an ounce of sense I would forget everything
If I really learned everything in Kindergarten
Then were the other twelve years necessary

School days of long mind numbing hours
Now there is another thought
Perhaps those twelve mean more than at first
Were they meant to give me something to think of
If that were true then why do I still think
To think of the learning there hurts me
Of all the world how can there be only one
A snow flake so fine there must be more alike
After all they pile so high on and on to the sky
They say there is a look alike somewhere for everyone
Why is this flake so special it has only one
If a tree falls in the woods
What an absurd question
No one was there how do you know if it fell
It fell it made a sound
At least when it hit the ground if nothing more
One train leaves from Chicago
What is that all about
Call the railroad unless you're the one making their schedule
Then call the trains and ask them to tell you
What if the bridge is washed out
What if one runs out of fuel or sand
What happens to those figures then
Right out the window of course
On things I have rambled on
Until endless is my musing
Of all the thoughts that run through me
How can I end this is what I am perplexed of now
Thoughts of things yet left un-thought
Thoughts of things I have not told you about
Perhaps I can return again to tell of them
Until then I am left with many, many various thoughts

Need

I lay in my empty bed
Thinking of my life
All those days running through my head
Making up the years that are my life

I close my eyes and try to sleep
Trying not to think of what I've done
But all I can do is weep
About the things I've yet to be done

My life incomplete
Days full of emptiness
The things I did not complete
My head is full of emptiness

People have come
People have gone
Which did I care as they came?
Which do I miss that have gone?

Where they have gone I do not know
Why they have gone I do not care
Now in my emptiness I want to know
Is my life that in need of care?

Corner of my Mind

In the corner of my mind
Stands a coat rack
Empty as my life is today
Where once hung many coats
From many different lives
Nothing hangs there now but dust
As each year passes it grows deeper
Soon I will be able to measure it
Gone are the coats that fit
And came to hang forever
Gone are the occasional coats
Those that would come and go
All of them gone now never to return
There are some that are gone
That I celebrate their leaving
Hoping; no pleading they never return
Even those in times like this
I wonder about from time to time
It is good that they are gone
So I have been told anyway
Some for the better
Even if I think it is not so
Some for the worse
Those are the ones I miss the most
Even though they will never return
I wonder if I should dust it off
To anticipate another one that fits
But I do nothing and the dust mounts
Perhaps I am happier the higher it is
But I cannot help but think why

Bottled up Inside

Twisted and turned around
Down inside all covered up
Becoming too deep to wade through
Lower the level to keep from drowning
Pour it in the dark brown bottles
Cap them as tight as possible
Label them individually with the pain
So they will not be forgotten
Peel off the labels like the others
Lock them all up with the rest
Someday maybe it can be opened
All the bottles taken out again
Sorted through and then divided
Small to large or large to small
It doesn't matter how they are sorted
In time maybe we can coup with it all
Open a bottle or two and throw a party
Or just smash them together at one time
Let the images and pain flow back in
What the hell it doesn't matter just now
Too much pain for now to bother
Until then it's all bottled up and locked away

Hope

Hope guides me through my day
Hope is what keeps me living
It's the hope of love
The hope of seeing you
Even if for just a moment
To take a leap of faith
Is to hope that there is faith
In all things there must be one
If there is no hope how can there be life
To live without it is not to live at all
Hope to dream or dream to hope
It the circle that we live
The hope of all things unknown
The hope of that which will come
It is that which is that keeps me going
This hope of things to come
This hope of what is to come
This hope of who is to come
This hope of you
That we will be together
Until then I live in my hope
To dream of your face
Until then I live with hope
That you also dream of mine
Until then I take my leap of faith
That hope is not lost on me
Until then I am full of hope
That faith is not lost in me
I hope to dream and dream of hope
That all will be as I dream

Thin Line

In the days of love and hate
We live our lives on the thin line
It takes from us and it give to us
All that we need to feel

Friends that come and go
Hatreds that go and come
It takes from us and gives to us
What a world this is

We wake we sleep
We breathe we suffocate
In this world of love and hate
We live our lives walking the line

Oh but for one friend
Oh but for one hatred
Where would we be without these
In this world of love and hate

I give to you a part of me
You give to me a part of you
Will it be love or will it be hate
We do not know until we part

No matter where we go
It does not escape us
Nor can we escape it
This line that haunts us

Call it what you will
It is what it always has been
And will always be
Love and hate

Forgive us if we hesitate
On all things of love and hate
It is just our nature
We live our lives on the thin line

Oh would we if we could
Stray from the thinness
Oh to walk a wider line
A line of enrichment perhaps

No matter it is all the same
Whichever line we choose
They are all crossed
Whether win or lose

In the days of love and hate
We live our lives on the thin line
Is it love or is it hate
We do not know until we part

So I ask this at the end
Why should we care
After all love is hate
And hate is love

W. M Stahl

Stranded or Forgotten

Stranded or forgotten does it matter
There is no way home just the same
Tossed away or tossed aside it doesn't matter
It comes to an end all the same

Down and out and away from home
The feeling of being left behind
Craving the need for safety and home
All one can do is look down the line

Rejected by everyone or everything
Doubt fills every part left empty or open
Like a piece of trash out the window with no wings
Cluttered about on the ground in the open

Worthless things to be tossed
Left alone with no way home
Not at all like things just lost
Yet all some can do is roam

Blossoms of Spring

Pink and yellow colors of spring
Pastels soft and new on the land
Bright days come again every year
Long winter nights soon forgotten
New birth pushes up from the ground
Springing forth into the growing light
Night and day near equal in time
Giving the earth a new chance to bloom
April comes as it always does in its own time
Snow will melt and the blossoms will sprout
Bringing forth the new life of spring
Birds sing and begin to make new nests
New families come out into the light
Animals of all kinds bringing new life
The world around changing daily
Gentle rains come and flowers grow
Brown grass to lush green lawn
New life is everywhere you look
Blossoms of spring bring smiles
Everywhere you look its true
Everywhere you look it's new
Nature works its magic on the earth
While the blossoms of spring work magic on us
Sweet scent of spring, carry me away
Blossoms of spring fill my eyes with spring
Fill my senses with everything that is spring

In My Mind

In my mind I can dream
There I can do anything
Live a life of purity
Or delve into the depths of depravity
Fight in battles long gone
Or those yet to come
Walk in ancient societies
And run with the dinosaurs
Yet in my mind is a more recent past
One that I am afraid is slipping away
In my mind I can
Sweep the floor in Philadelphia
At the signing of the declaration of independence
Serve beer as Paul Revere rode into the night
Worked the docks
At Boston Harbor during the "Tea Party"
Stand up when they killed Nathan Hale
As I too "regret that I have but one life to give my country"
Listened in as Patrick Henry spoke
And repeated "Give me Liberty or give me death"
Be a fisherman rowing the boat
Carrying Washington across the Delaware
Sit with the writers of the Constitution
And read as they write the freedoms of the press
And of our right as Americans to bear arms
Stand next to Lincoln
As he speaks in Gettysburg
Oh let me not forget that I can be with every American
In every battle ever fought for freedoms around the world
In my mind I can be at all of these places whenever I wish
Yet in this world come forces
Forces of change that wish to take this gift away
Oh they say it will be good for the country
This change and the taking away
Yet it is no good for us or our Constitution

This piece of paper hallowed and revered
Will be just paper in our past if they have their way
And your arms will be given away
Along with many other rights
The nanny state has begun to take control
Is this what they had in mind
Those that gave all for us
Those that risked all for US
In my mind I can be in any of these places and more
But if we keep silent much longer
As our country is sold down the river
All in the name of who knows what
The only place we may be able to speak of these things
Will be in our minds......
Let not our ancestors struggle go out with a whimper
Fight its ending if not for you for those that come after
That they do not have to know freedoms only in their minds

Glory

What would you do for glory?
A question asked but to a few
One that usually ends with a death
What price glory
What makes a hero?
Aren't we all a hero to some?
If only for a moment
For that instant you were a hero
To someone you made their world
Fixed the flat or said the right word
Answered a question that changed a life
Made a difference in someone's day
In our minds the glory or the need
Which do we know first?
The need is the reason that we act
Glory is its reward?
We do it all for the glory?
We do it all for love
The love of each other
Man Woman Child
Brother Sister Lover
Father Mother other
The glory is the aftermath

Choices, the good, the bad, the ugly

We all make a choice each and every day
Some good some bad in each and everyway
Yet make them we must
Even the ones we distrust

I made one so many days ago
That I knew was not the right way to go
Yet I made it just the same
Even though I knew it was totally insane

I was not the only one
We each made the wrong one
Our choice was made one faithful day
We both knew there would come another day

Many years since has come and gone
How I have wish I had not done what was done
Stood by the choice as said I would
I wanted to take it back each day oh how I wish I could

We live by our choices right or wrong
We cannot go back if we made it wrong
Forward we must go on as time will not stop
Even when in our mind we know it has to stop

What was done was done
But it was not good for everyone
Now out it all comes
The day I prayed would come

Finally I hope I make it right
Please god, help me get this one right
The choice was made though it hurt each one
I hope in your heart you can forgive us each one

What to Say

I hoped and prayed the time would come
That I can say what I want to say
It is not easy to tell of this that was done
No it was not easy in anyway
I did what I did to keep from causing troubles
I thought about it for so many days
All the hate and discontent that it would bring
It would have happened either way
So I chose this bad thing over the other
And hoped I could make it right someday
I knew that it would haunt me
Yet I lived with it every day
It was what I promised after all
Something I regret in every way
I saw you once when you were little
I remember it to this very day
Yes it was so hard to see you go
But I turned away
I made the choice the die was cast
Even though it hurt me more everyday
It may have gotten easier
But the pain never went away
I longed to hold and care for you
I could not help but think of you every day
I wondered if somewhere you needed me
I hoped that I could tell you someday
Words escape me every time I think of it
Could I ever make it right by what I would say?
Just how do you tell of things that need telling?
Especially as time slips by more everyday
I can only hope for your understanding
I never once thought of what you might say
Perhaps even reject me before it was all said
Hopefully it will not be that way

I always hoped that when the time was right
I would know just what to say
That day may grow closer and yet may come
But still I know not what to say
One can only hope that you will forgive me
That is all that I can pray
No matter what you do or how you react
Know that I have loved you each and everyday

W. M Stahl

I hope you have enjoyed your little trip into my world of poems and mind. Some things I am sure made great sense while others, perhaps not so much. I have never promised to make perfect sense to anyone with my writing, including myself. I am sure I will never be mistaken for someone with great philosophical ideals and thoughts. I consider that a great relief as that would be too great a title to uphold. The thought of it along with whose company I would be keeping and compared to is quite frightening to say the least.

www.ingramcontent.com/pod-product-compliance
Lightning Source LLC
Chambersburg PA
CBHW071834020426
42331CB00007B/1728